AFTER MAGRITTE

After Magritte

TOM STOPPARD

FABER AND FABER
London · Boston

First published in 1971
by Faber and Faber Limited
3 Queen Square London WC1
Reprinted 1973, 1975 and 1978
Printed in Great Britain by
Whitstable Litho Ltd Whitstable Kent
All rights reserved

ISBN 0 571 09657 3

The first performance of AFTER MAGRITTE was given at the Ambiance Lunch-hour Theatre Club on 9th April 1970. The cast was as follows:

FOOT	Clive Barker
HOLMES	Malcolm Ingram
HARRIS	Stephen Moore
THELMA	Prunella Scales
MOTHER	Josephine Tewson

Directed by Geoffrey Reeves

Characters

HARRIS   aged about 40
THELMA his wife, a bit younger, attractive
MOTHER a little old, tough, querulous lady
FOOT   Detective Inspector
HOLMES Police Constable

SCENE

A room. Early evening.

The only light is that which comes through the large window which is facing the audience. The street door is in the same upstage wall. There is another door on each side of the stage, leading to the rest of the flat.

The central ceiling light hangs from a long flex which disappears up into the flies. The lampshade itself is a heavy metal hemisphere, opaque, poised about eight feet from the floor.

A yard or more to one side (Stage L), and similarly hanging from the flies, is a fruit basket attractively overflowing with apples, oranges, bananas, pineapple, and grapes. The cord or flex is tied round the handle of the basket.

It will become apparent that the light fixture is on a counterweight system; it can be raised or lowered, or kept in any vertical position, by means of the counterbalance, which in this case is a basket of fruit.

Most of the furniture is stacked up against the street door in a sort of barricade. An essential item is a long low bench-type table, about eight feet long, but the pile also includes a settee, two comfortable chairs, a TV set, a cupboard and a wind-up gramophone with an old-fashioned horn. The cupboard is probably the item on which stand the telephone and

9

a deep-shaded table lamp, unlit but connected to a wall plug.

Directly under the central light is a wooden chair. Hanging over the back of the chair is a black tail-coat, a white dress shirt and a white bow-tie. Towards Stage R, in profile, is an ironing board with its iron upended on the asbestos mat at the centre-stage end of the board.

There is no other furniture.

There are three people in the room.

MOTHER *is lying on her back on the ironing board, her head to Stage R, her downstage foot up against the flat of the iron. A white bath towel covers her from ankle to chin. Her head and part of her face are concealed in a tight-fitting black rubber bathing cap. A black bowler hat reposes on her stomach. She could be dead; but is not.*

THELMA HARRIS *is dressed in a full-length ballgown and her hair is expensively "up". She looks as though she is ready to go out to a dance, which she is. Her silver shoes, however, are not on her feet: they have been discarded somewhere on the floor.* THELMA *is discovered on her hands and knees, in profile to the audience, staring at the floor ahead and giving vent to an occasional sniff.*

REGINALD HARRIS *is standing on the wooden chair. His torso is bare, but underneath his thigh-length green rubber fishing waders he wears his black evening dress trousers. His hands are at his sides. His head is tilted back directly below the lampshade, which hangs a foot or two above him and he is blowing slowly and deliberately up into the recess of the shade.*

Gazing at this scene through the window is a uniformed

10

Police Constable (HOLMES). *Only his shoulders, his face and his helmet are visible above the sill. He stands absolutely motionless, and might be a cut-out figure; but is not.*

For several seconds there is no movement, and no sound save the occasional blowing from HARRIS *and the occasional sniffing from* THELMA. THELMA *pads forward a couple of paces, still scanning the floor ahead and around.* HARRIS *blows into the lampshade.*

Without looking up at HARRIS, THELMA *speaks.*

THELMA: It's electric, dear.

HARRIS: (*mildly*) I didn't think it was a flaming torch.

THELMA: There's no need to use language. That's what I always say.

(*She pads on a bit, scanning the floor.* HARRIS *tries to remove the light bulb but it is apparently still too hot: he blows on his sharply withdrawn fingers, and then continues to blow on the light bulb. After a couple of blows he tests the bulb again and is able to remove it.*)

(*This upsets the delicate balance of the counterweight. The shade, relieved of the weight of the bulb, slowly begins to ascend, while the basket of fruit descends accordingly.* HARRIS, *however, has anticipated this and the movement is one of only a few inches before he has turned on his chair and removed an apple from the basket. This reverses the effect: the basket ascends, the shade descends. But* HARRIS *has anticipated this also:*

11

he takes a bite out of the apple and replaces it.
The equilibrium is thus restored.)
You could have used your handkerchief.

HARRIS: (*intrigued*) You mean, *semaphor*?

(*But* THELMA *is not listening: she has given up her*
search, stood up, approached her shoes—and
stepped on something; it is in fact a lead slug
from a .22 calibre pistol. She picks it up with
satisfaction and tosses it into a metal wastebin
wherein it makes the appropriate sound.)

THELMA: A hundred and forty-nine.

(*She hands the iron's plug up to* HARRIS *and*
accepts from him the warm bulb.)

HARRIS: I never took semaphor as a sophomore, morse
the pity.

(THELMA *looks at him icily but he has his own*
cool.) I used the time in a vain attempt to get the
Rockefeller girl to marry me for my sense of
humour. Would you pass my hat?

(THELMA *passes him the bowler hat, which he*
puts on his head. He then inserts the iron plug
into the light socket, deftly removing his hat and
hanging it on a banana, thus cancelling out the
imbalance threatened by the weight of the plug
and its flex. THELMA's *attention does not stay to*
be impressed.)

THELMA: For some reason, my mind keeps returning to
that one-legged footballer we passed in the car.
. . . What *position* do you suppose he plays?

12

(HARRIS *has got down off the chair and looked critically around.*)

HARRIS: Bit dark in here.

(*The natural light from the window is indeed somewhat inadequate.* THELMA *pursues her own thoughts and a path to the light switch, positioned by the door at Stage* L, *which controls the ceiling light, or, at the moment, the iron.*)

THELMA: I keep thinking about him. What guts he must have!

HARRIS: Put the light on.

(THELMA *independently depresses the light switch, and the red warm-up light on the iron comes on.* HARRIS *regards it sceptically.*)

Most unsatisfactory.

THELMA: I mean, what fantastic *pluck*! What real never-say-die *spirit*, you know what I mean? (*Pause.*) Bloody unfair on the rest of the team, mind you —you'd think the decent thing would have been to hang up his boot. *What are you doing now?!* (*For* HARRIS *has gone upstage to the table lamp resting amid the barricade and tried, without result, to turn it on, whereupon he has started to blow violently against the shade. He replies immediately.*)

HARRIS: Filthy. Hasn't been dusted for weeks. I could write my name on it.

(*He proceeds to do so, in full, remarking the while:*)

13

It wasn't a football, it was a turtle.

THELMA: A turtle?

HARRIS: Or a large tortoise.

THELMA: *What?*

HARRIS: He was carrying a tortoise.

THELMA: You must be blind.

HARRIS: (*equably*) It was he who was blind. What
happened to the bulb?

(*He means the bulb from the table lamp.*
THELMA *however, holds out the warm bulb.*)

THELMA: Here.

HARRIS: What did you take the bulb out for?

THELMA: No, that was the one you put in the bathroom.
This is the one which——

(*As he takes the bulb from her by the metal end
and flips it angrily into the air, catching it by the
glass.*)

——you just took out——

HARRIS: (*shouts*) Not by the metal end!

(*Irritably he goes to insert the bulb into the
table lamp.*)

THELMA: And how do you explain the West Bromwich
Albion football shirt?

HARRIS: Pyjamas—he was wearing pyjamas.

(*He successfully switches on the lamp, raising the
gloom considerably as he gazes moodily around.
He continues to speak, characteristically, without
punctuation.*)

This place is run like a madhouse. What's that

14

policeman staring at?

(THELMA *turns to the window, marches up to it and viciously draws the curtains together.*)

THELMA: Bloody nerve!

(*There is a piercing scream, from* MOTHER *as she jerks her foot away from the heated-up iron. This causes some confusion and cries of pain from* MOTHER *and cries of "Mother!" from* THELMA *who snatches up the iron and places it on the wooden chair, the fruit adjusting itself accordingly.* MOTHER *is now sitting up on the ironing board, facing the audience, her burned foot clutched in her lap, the other hanging down. Her first audible word seems to be a vulgarity; but is not.*)

MOTHER: *Butter!*

THELMA: (*primly*) Now there's no need to use language——

MOTHER: Get some butter!

THELMA: *Butter!*—Get butter, Reginald!

(HARRIS *rushes out.* THELMA *grabs the phone.*)

(*Dialling.*) Don't move—whatever you do don't move—Hello!—I want an ambulance!

(*There is a loud knocking on the door.* THELMA *drops the phone (it falls into the cradle) and rushes to the window, shouting.*)

Who is it?

(*She draws back the curtains, and the Policeman reappears.*)

15

HOLMES: It's the police!

THELMA: (*furiously*) I asked for an ambulance!
(*She viciously draws the curtains together and dashes back to pick up the phone.*)
(HARRIS *rushes in with half a pound of soft butter on a butter dish.*)

HARRIS: Where do you want it, mother?

MOTHER: On my foot, you nincompoop.
(HARRIS *slams the butter up against the sole of* MOTHER's *undamaged foot.*)
(*The confusion ceases at once.* THELMA *replaces the phone and stands quietly.* HARRIS *stands up looking slightly crestfallen.* MOTHER *regards him glacially. There is a silence.*)
You married a fool, Thelma.
(MOTHER *gets down on the floor, on her good, though buttered, foot.*)
Has the bathroom light been repaired?

HARRIS: I put in a new bulb, mother.

MOTHER: I hope you cleaned your boots.
(MOTHER *hops one-legged across the stage to the door and leaves, not before delivering the following threat.*)
I shall be back for my practice.
(*Certain things are integrated with the following dialogue.*)
(*The iron goes back on the ironing board. The fruit adjusts.*)
(THELMA *irons the white dress shirt while* HARRIS,

16

sitting on the wooden chair, takes off his waders, which have been concealing not only his trousers but his black patent leather shoes. HARRIS *crams the waders into the cupboard in the barricade of furniture.*)

(*When the shirt has been ironed,* HARRIS *puts it on, and puts on the bow-tie, and finally the coat. After ironing,* HARRIS *climbs back on the wooden chair to remove the iron plug and, of course, the bowler hat, which, for want of anywhere else, he puts on his head.*)

(MOTHER *leaves the room.*)

HARRIS: Don't start blaming me. She could have lain on the floor.

THELMA: Oh yes—very nice—with my back in the state it's in—you'd rather I bent double.

HARRIS: You could have squatted over her. It's not *my* fault that the furniture could not be put to its proper use in its proper place.

THELMA: *If* you're referring to the Cricklewood Lyceum——

HARRIS: I *am* referring to the Cricklewood Lyceum—it was a fiasco——

THELMA: You know perfectly well that my foot got caught in my hem——

HARRIS: With *your* legs?—your feet don't *reach* your hem.

THELMA: My legs are insured for £5,000!

HARRIS: Only against theft. The fact of the matter is, it

was a botch from first to last, and that is why we find ourselves having to go through it again at the eleventh hour, half of which has now gone. *We are never going to get away on time!*

THELMA: (*ironing the shirt*) I am being as quick as I can. All I can say is I'll be glad when it's all over and things are back to normal. It's making you short-tempered and argumentative. You contradict everything I say——

HARRIS: (*heatedly*) *That* I deny——

THELMA: I've only got to mention that the footballer had a football under his arm and you start insisting it was a tortoise. Why a footballer should play with a tortoise is a question which you don't seem prepared to face.

HARRIS: (*calmingly, reasonably*) Look—he was not a footballer. He was just a chap in striped pyjamas. It was a perfectly natural, not to say uninteresting, mistake and it led you to the further and even more boring misapprehension that what he was carrying was a football—whereas *I*——

THELMA: Whereas you, accepting as a matter of course a pyjama-clad figure in the street, leap to the natural conclusion that he must be carrying a tortoise.

HARRIS: The man obviously had his reasons.

THELMA: You've got to admit that a football is more likely.

HARRIS: More likely?

THELMA: In the sense that there would be more footballs than tortoises in a built-up area.

HARRIS: Leaving aside the fact that your premise is far from self-evident, it is more *likely*, by that criterion, that what the fellow had under his arm was a Christmas pudding or a copy of Whitaker's Almanac, but I happened to see him with my own eyes——

THELMA: We all saw him——

HARRIS: —and he was an old man with one leg and a white beard, dressed in pyjamas, hopping along in the rain with a tortoise under his arm and brandishing a white stick to clear a path through those gifted with sight——

THELMA: There was no one else on the pavement.

HARRIS: Since he was blind he could hardly be expected to know that.

THELMA: Who said he was blind? *You* say so——

HARRIS: (*heatedly*) He had a white stick, woman!

THELMA: (*equably*) In my opinion it was an ivory cane.

HARRIS: (*shouting*) An ivory cane IS a white stick!!
(*This seems to exhaust them both.* THELMA *irons placidly, though still rebellious. After a while....*)

THELMA: (*scornfully*) Pyjamas . . . I suppose he was hopping in his sleep. Yes, I can see it now—a bad dream—he leaps to his foot, grabs his tortoise and feels his way into the street——

HARRIS: I am only telling you what I saw! And I suggest

to you that a blind one-legged white-bearded
footballer would have a hard time keeping his
place in West Bromwich Albion

THELMA: He was a young chap.

HARRIS: (*patiently*) He had a white beard.

THELMA: Shaving foam.

HARRIS: (*leaping up*) Have you taken leave of your
senses?

THELMA: (*strongly*) It was shaving foam! In pyjamas, if you
insist, striped in the colours of West Bromwich
Albion, if you allow, carrying under his arm, if
not a football then something very similar like
a wineskin or a pair of bagpipes, and swinging a
white stick in the form of an ivory cane——

HARRIS: Bagpipes?

THELMA: —*but what he had on his face was definitely
shaving foam!* (*Pause.*) Or possibly some kind of
yashmak.

(HARRIS *is almost speechless.*)

HARRIS: The most—*the very most*—I am prepared to
concede is that he *may* have been a sort of
street arab making off with his lute—*but young
he was not and white-bearded he was!*

THELMA: His *loot*?

HARRIS: (*expansively*) Or his mandolin—Who's to say?

THELMA: You admit he could have been musical?

HARRIS: I admit nothing of the sort! As a matter of fact,
if he had been an Arab musician, the likelihood
is that he would have been carrying a gourd—

20

which is very much the shape and size of a tortoise, which strongly suggests that I was right in my initial conjecture: white beard, white stick, pyjamas, tortoise. I refuse to discuss it any further.

THELMA: You'll never admit you're wrong, will you?

HARRIS: On the contrary, if I were ever wrong I would be the *first* to admit it. But these outlandish embellishments of yours are gratuitous and strain the credulity.

THELMA: (*sighing*) We should have stopped and taken a photograph. Then we wouldn't be having these arguments.

HARRIS: (*morosely*) We wouldn't be having them if we'd stayed at home, as I myself wished to do.

THELMA: It was for mother's benefit, not yours. She doesn't often ask to be taken anywhere, and it didn't cost you much to let her have her pleasure.

HARRIS: It cost me ten shillings in parking tickets alone.

THELMA: It was only one ticket, and it was your own fault for not putting any money in the meter. The truth is that we are very fortunate that a woman of her age still has an active interest, even if it is the tuba.

HARRIS: Active interest?—she's an obsessed woman; dragging us half way across London—you'd think having one in the house and playing it morning, noon and night would be enough for anyone. It's certainly too much for me.

THELMA: She's entitled to practise, just as much as we are.

HARRIS: But it's our house.

THELMA: You shouldn't have asked her to move in if you felt like that.

HARRIS: It was your idea.

THELMA: You agreed to it.

HARRIS: I agreed to her living out her last days among her loved ones—I said nothing about having her underfoot for half a lifetime.

THELMA: You said it would be useful for baby-sitting.

HARRIS: We haven't got any *children*!

THELMA: That's hardly her fault. (*Pause.*) Or mine.

(HARRIS *gets slowly to his feet.*)

HARRIS: How dare you? How *dare* you! Right—that's it! I've put up with a lot of slanders but my indulgence is now at an end. This is my house and you can tell your mother to pack her tuba and get out!

THELMA: But, Reginald——

HARRIS: No—you have pushed me too far. When I married you I didn't expect to have your mother——

THELMA: (*shouting back at him*) She's not my mother— she's *your* mother!

HARRIS: (*immediately*) *Rubbish!*

(*However, he sits down rather suddenly.*)

(*calmer*) My mother is a . . . tall . . . aristocratic

22

woman, in a red mac . . . answers to the name
of . . .

THELMA: That's your Aunt——

THELMA:⎱
HARRIS:⎰ ——Jessica.

(HARRIS *stands up and sits down immediately. His
manner is agitated. He is by now fully dressed.*)
(THELMA *folds the ironing board and takes it out
of the room.*)
(MOTHER *enters, from her bath, robed or dressed,
without the bathing cap, but still hopping on one
foot. She hops across the room.*)

MOTHER: The bulb in the bathroom's gone again.

(*She leaves by the other door.* HARRIS *gets up and
goes to the cupboard, extracting his waders.*
MOTHER *returns, hopping, carrying a large felt
bag.*)

I let the water out.

(HARRIS *stuffs the waders back into the cupboard.
He moves towards the door, but is most unsettled.
He halts, turns and addresses his* MOTHER, *who is
now on the wooden chair.*)

HARRIS: (*rather aggressively*) Would you like a cup of
tea, Mum?

(*The old lady is startled by the appellation. She
looks up, straight ahead, then turns to look at*
HARRIS *in a resentful manner.* HARRIS *quails. He
turns and is about to leave again when there is a
loud knocking on the street door.*)

23

(MOTHER *continues fiddling with the felt bag,
from which, at this moment she withdraws her
tuba.* HARRIS *with the air of a man more kicked
against than kicking, approaches the pile of
furniture and begins to take it apart as* MOTHER
puts the tuba to her lips.)

(MOTHER *plays while* HARRIS *moves the furniture
piece by piece into its proper place. Before he has
finished,* THELMA *enters with a drink in one hand
and a flower vase in the other. She puts them
down and helps* HARRIS *with the heavier pieces.*)

(*The long, low table is placed centrally under the
lampshade. The settee goes behind it and a comfortable chair goes either side. This is managed
so that* MOTHER *does not have to move from her
position on the wooden chair, or desist from
playing her jaunty tune, until the last stages, just
before the police enter. When they do so*
(INSPECTOR FOOT *and* PC HOLMES), *everything is
in place, the wooden chair put back against the
wall, and the three people seated comfortably.*
THELMA *smoking and holding her drink; the tuba
out of view, perhaps behind* MOTHER'*s chair.*)

(*The only surviving oddity is the fruit basket,
when the door is finally flung open and* FOOT
charges into the room, right downstage, with
HOLMES *taking up position in a downstage corner
and naturally looking a little taken aback.*)

FOOT: What is the meaning of this bizarre spectacle?!!

(*Pause. They all squint about.*)

THELMA: The counterweight fell down and broke. Is that a crime?

(*FOOT clasps both hands behind his back and goes into an aggressive playing-for-time stroll, passing* HOLMES.)

(*FOOT speaks out of the corner of his mouth.*)

FOOT: Got the right house, have you?

HOLMES: Yes, sir.

(*FOOT continues his stroll.* HARRIS *would like to help.*)

MOTHER: (*uncertainly*) Is it all right for me to practice?

(*FOOT ignores her, his eyes darting desperately about until they fix on the table-lamp.* FOOT *stops dead. His head moves slightly, along the line of the lampshade reading the words scrawled on it.*)

FOOT: (*trimphantly*) Reginald William Harris?

HARRIS: Thirty-seven Mafeking Villas.

FOOT: You are addressing a police officer not an envelope. Would you kindly answer my questions in the right order.

HARRIS: I'm sorry.

(*FOOT turns his back on* HARRIS, *denoting a fresh start, and barks.*)

FOOT: Reginald William Harris!

HARRIS: Here.

FOOT: Where do you live?—*you're doing it again!!!*

MOTHER: Who is that man?

FOOT: I am Chief Inspector Foot.

(HARRIS *rises to his feet with a broad enchanted smile.*)

HARRIS: Not Foot of the Y——

FOOT: (*screams*) Silence!

(FOOT *starts travelling again, keeping his agitation almost under control, ignoring* MOTHER'*s murmur.*)

MOTHER: Can I practice now?

(FOOT *arrives at* HOLMES, *and addresses him out of the corner of his mouth.*)

FOOT: Quite sure? You never mentioned the fruit.

HOLMES: (*plaintively*) There was so much else. . . .

FOOT: Better have a look round.

HOLMES: Yes, sir.

(THELMA *ignores the convention of the "aside", raising her voice and her head.*)

THELMA: I'm afraid things are a bit of a mess.

FOOT: (*briskly*) I can't help that. You know what they say—clean knickers every day, you never know when you might be run over. Well it's happened to you on a big scale.

(HARRIS *regains his feet.*)

HARRIS: Just a minute. Have you got a search warrant?

(HOLMES *pauses.*)

FOOT: Yes.

HARRIS: Can I see it?

FOOT: I can't put my hand to it at the moment.

HARRIS: (*incredulous*) You can't *find* your search warrant!

26

FOOT: (*smoothly*) I had it about my person when I
came in. I may have dropped it. Have a look
round, Holmes.

(THELMA *rises to her feet with a broad enchanted
smile.*)

THELMA: *Not——*

FOOT: (*screams*) Be quiet!

(THELMA *sits down.* HARRIS *will not.*)

HARRIS: Now look here——

FOOT: Can I see your television licence?

(HARRIS *freezes with his mouth open. After a long
moment he closes it.*)

HARRIS: (*vaguely*) Er, it must be about . . . somewhere . . .

FOOT: Good. While you're looking for your television
licence, Holmes will look for the search
warrant.

(HARRIS *sits down thoughtfully.*)

(*To* HOLMES.) It could have blown about a bit
or slipped down under the floorboards.

HOLMES: Right, sir.

(HOLMES *begins to crawl around the room.*)

MOTHER: Is it all right for me to practice?

(FOOT *ignores her. He stands looking down
smugly at* HARRIS.)

FOOT: Yes, I expect you're wondering what gave you
away.

HARRIS: (*wanly*) Was it one of those detector vans?

(*But* FOOT *is already on the move.*)

27

FOOT: Well, I'll tell you. It's a simple tale—no hot tips from Interpol, no days and nights of keeping watch in the rain, no trouser turn-ups hoovered by Forensics or undercover agents selling the *Evening News* in Chinatown—no!—just a plain ordinary copper on his beat! Yes! —the PC is still the best tool the Yard has got!——

(HOLMES *is behind him, on his hands and knees.*)

HOLMES: Excuse me, sir.

FOOT: (*irritated*) Not in here; *around.*

HOLMES: (*getting to his feet*) Yes, sir. Is this anything, sir?

(*He hands* FOOT *a .22 lead slug which he has found on the floor.* FOOT *accepts it unheedingly; he is already talking.* HOLMES *leaves the room.*)

FOOT: He's not one of your TV heroes, young Holmes—he's just a young man doing his job and doing it well—sometimes not seeing his kids—Dean, five, and Sharon, three—for days on end—often getting home after his wife's asleep and back on the beat before she wakes— tireless, methodical, eagle-eyed—always ready with a friendly word for the old lag crossing the road or sixpence for the old lady trying to go straight——

(HOLMES *has re-entered the room and has been dogging* FOOT's *footsteps, waiting for an opportunity to speak, which he now deduces, wrongly, has presented itself.*)

HOLMES: To tell you the truth, sir, I'm not absolutely
sure what a search warrant looks like. . . .
(*But* FOOT *marches on, round the right-angle of
the room, while* HOLMES *plods stolidly on and out
without changing course. As* FOOT *moves he is
weighing and jiggling in his hand the lead slug,
and he has been becoming more aware of its
presence there.*)

FOOT: Yes, that's the sort of metal that has brought
you to book.
(FOOT *absently examines the object in his hand.
He seems surprised at finding it there.*)
When Holmes got back to the station and
described to me the scene he had witnessed
through your window, I realized he had
stumbled on something even bigger than
even. . . .
(*He tails off, and whirls on them, holding up the
metal slug.*)
Do any of you know what this is?
(THELMA *holds up her hand.*)
Well?
(THELMA *gets up and takes the slug out of* FOOT'S
hand.)

THELMA: It's a lead slug from a .22 calibre pistol. Thank
you.
(*She tosses the slug into the metal bin wherein
it makes the appropriate sound.*)

A hundred and fifty.

(*She returns to her seat.* FOOT *walks over to the metal bin and peers into it. He bends and takes out a handful of lead slugs and lets them fall back. He stoops again and comes up with the broken halves of the porcelain container that had held the slugs and acted as the counterweight to the light fitting. He regards the basket of fruit. He drops the debris back into the bin. He addresses himself to* THELMA.)

FOOT: It is my duty to tell you that I am not satisfied with your reply.

THELMA: What was the question?

FOOT: That is hardly the point.

THELMA: Ask me another.

FOOT: Very well. Why did it take you so long to answer the door?

THELMA: The furniture was piled up against it.

FOOT: (*sneeringly*) Really? Expecting visitors, Mrs. Harris?

THELMA: On the contrary.

FOOT: In my experience your conduct usually indicates that visitors are expected.

THELMA: I am prepared to defend myself against any logician you care to produce.

FOOT: (*snaps*) Do you often stack the furniture up against the door?

THELMA: Yes. Is that a crime?

FOOT: (*furiously*) Will you stop trying to exploit my

professional knowledge for your private ends!—
I didn't do twenty years of hard grind to have
my brains picked by every ignorant layman who
finds out I'm a copper!

(HARRIS *has relapsed into a private brood, from
which this outburst rouses him. He has decided
to capitulate. He stands up.*)

HARRIS: All right! Can we call off this game of cat and
mouse?! I haven't *got* a television licence—I
kept meaning to get one but somehow. . . .
(FOOT *turns to him.*)

FOOT: Then perhaps you have a diploma from the
Royal College of Surgeons.

HARRIS: (*taken aback*) I'm afraid not. I didn't realize
they were compulsory.

FOOT: (*without punctuation*) I have reason to believe
that within the last hour in this room you
performed without anaesthetic an illegal
operation on a bald nigger minstrel about
five-foot-two or Pakistani and that is only the
beginning!

HARRIS: I deny it!

FOOT: Furthermore, that this is a disorderly house!

HARRIS: *That* I admit—Thelma, I've said it before and
I'll say it again——

THELMA: (*shouting angrily*) Don't you come that with me!
—what with the dancing, the travelling, ironing
your shirts, massaging your mother and starting
all over every morning, I haven't got time to

wipe my nose!

HARRIS: (*equally roused*) *That's* what I want to talk to you about—sniff-sniff—it's a disgusting habit in a woman——

THELMA: (*shouting*) All right—so I've got a cold!—(*Turning to the world, which happens to be in the direction of* FOOT)—Is that a crime?

FOOT: (*hysterically*) I will not warn you again! (*He patrols furiously.*) The disorderliness I was referring to consists of immoral conduct—tarted-up harpies staggering about drunk to the wide, naked men in rubber garments hanging from the lampshade—Have you got a music licence? (*As he passes the gramophone.*)

HARRIS: There is obviously a perfectly logical reason for everything.

FOOT: There is, and I mean to make it stick! What was the nature of this operation? (FOOT *finds himself staring at a line of single greasy footprints leading across the room. He hops along the trail, fascinated, until he reaches the door to* MOTHER's *bath. He turns.*) (*Quietly.*) The D.P.P. is going to take a very poor view if you have been offering cut-price amputations to immigrants. (HOLMES *enters excitedly with the ironing board.*)

HOLMES: Sir!

FOOT: That's an ironing board.

HOLMES: (*instantaneously demoralized*) Yes, sir.

FOOT: What we're looking for is a darkie short of a leg or two.

HOLMES: (*retiring*) Right, sir.

MOTHER: Is it all right for me to practice?

FOOT: No, it is not all right! Ministry standards may be lax but we draw the line at Home Surgery to bring in the little luxuries of life.

MOTHER: I only practice on the tuba.

FOOT: Tuba, femur, fibula—it takes more than a penchant for rubber gloves to get a licence nowadays.

MOTHER: The man's quite mad.

FOOT: That's what they said at the station when I sent young Holmes to take a turn down Mafeking Villas, but everything I have heard about events here today convinces me that you are up to your neck in the Crippled Minstrel Caper!

THELMA: Is that a dance?

HARRIS: My wife and I are always on the look-out for novelty numbers. We're prepared to go out on a limb if it's not in bad taste.

FOOT: (*shouting him down*) Will you kindly stop interrupting while I am about to embark on my exegesis!! (*Pauses, he collects himself.*) The story begins about lunchtime today. The facts appear to be that shortly after two o'clock this afternoon, the talented though handicapped doyen of the Victoria Palace Happy Minstrel Troupe

33

emerged from his dressing-room in blackface, and entered the sanctum of the box-office staff; whereupon, having broken his crutch over the heads of those good ladies, the intrepid uniped made off with the advance takings stuffed into the crocodile boot which, it goes without saying, he had surplus to his conventional requirements.

HARRIS: It must have been a unique moment in the annals of crime.

FOOT: Admittedly, the scene as I have described it is as yet my own reconstruction based on an eye-witness account of the man's flight down nearby Ponsonby Place, where, it is my firm conjecture, Harris, he was driven off by accomplices in a fast car. They might have got away with it had it not been for an elderly lady residing at number seven, who, having nothing to do but sit by her window and watch the world go by, saw flash by in front of her eyes a bizarre and desperate figure. Being herself an old devotee of minstrel shows she recognized him at once for what he was. She was even able to glimpse his broken crutch, the sort of detail that speaks volumes to an experienced detective. By the time she had made her way to her front door, the street was deserted, save for one or two tell-tale coins on the pavement. Nevertheless, it was her report which enabled me to reconstruct the sequence

34

of events—though I am now inclined to modify the details inasmuch as the culprit may have been a genuine coloured man impersonating a minstrel in order to insinuate himself into the side door to the box office. These are just the broad strokes. My best man, Sergeant Potter, is at this moment checking the Victoria Palace end of the case and I am confidently expecting verification by telephone of my hypothesis. In any event I think you now understand why I am here.

HARRIS: No, I'm afraid I'm completely at a loss.

FOOT: Then perhaps you can explain what your car was doing in Ponsonby Place at twenty-five minutes past two this afternoon.

HARRIS: So that's it.

FOOT: Exactly. It was bad luck getting that parking ticket, Harris—one of those twists of fate that have cracked many an alibi. We traced your car and sent Constable Holmes to take a look at you.

HARRIS: But we know nothing of this outrage.

FOOT: What were you doing there, right across London?

HARRIS: We went to see an exhibition of surrealistic art at the Tate Gallery.

FOOT: I must say that in a lifetime of off-the-cuff alibis I have seldom been moved closer to open derision.

THELMA: Perhaps it would help to explain that my mother-in-law is a devotee of Maigret.

MOTHER: *Magritte.*

FOOT: I'm afraid I don't follow your drift.

HARRIS: You will when I tell you that she is an accomplished performer on, and passionate admirer in all its aspects, of the tuba.

FOOT: Tuba? (*Angrily.*) You are stretching my patience and my credulity to breaking poi—— (*He sees* MOTHER *with the tuba now on her lap.*)

MOTHER: Can I have a go now?

HARRIS: Hearing that among the canvasses on view were several depicting the instrument of her chief and indeed obsessional interest, my wife's mother, in law, or rather my mother, prevailed upon us to take her to the exhibition, which we did, notwithstanding the fact that we could ill afford the time from rehearsing for a professional engagement at the North Circular Dancerama tonight, and to which, I may say, we will shortly have to absent ourselves. (*To* THELMA *without pause.*) Have you taken up your hem?

(THELMA *gasps with dismay and self-reproach and immediately whips off her dress. This leaves her in bra and panties. Her action, since it is not especially remarkable, is not especially remarked upon.* THELMA's *preoccupation now is to find needle and thread, in which she succeeds quite*

36

quickly without leaving the room. However, her chief problem during the ensuing minutes is her lack of a tailor's dummy. She tries draping the dress over various bits of furniture, and tackling the hem, but for one reason or another—the inadequate lighting or the lowness of the chairs, etc.—she is intermittently frustrated until, quite naturally and smoothly, she drapes the dress over HARRIS, *who simply takes no notice; indeed* THELMA *is reduced to following him on her hands and knees between stitches, and occasionally asking him to keep still. Needless to say, the dress must be sleeveless and full.*)

(*There has been no pause in the dialogue.*)

Look at her!—with an organized partner I could have reached the top!

FOOT: About your alibi——

MOTHER: It was rubbish.

FOOT: Hah!

(*He turns to her.*)

MOTHER: Tubas on fire, tubas stuck to lions and naked women, tubas hanging in the sky—there was one woman with a tuba with a sack over her head as far as I could make out. I doubt he'd ever tried to play one; in fact if you ask me the man must have been some kind of lunatic.

HARRIS: As my mother says, the visit was a disappointment.

THELMA: I must say I have to agree. I don't like to speak

37

slightingly of another artiste, but it just wasn't life-like—I'm not saying it wasn't *good*—well *painted*—but not from life, you know?

FOOT: That has no bearing on the case. Did you see anybody you knew at the exhibition?

MOTHER: I saw Sir Adrian Boult.

FOOT: Would he be prepared to come forward?

HARRIS: You'll have to forgive the old lady. She sees Sir Adrian Boult everywhere.

MOTHER: I saw him in Selfridges.

FOOT: Yes, quite——

MOTHER: He was buying a cushion-cover.

FOOT: (*loudly*) Can we please keep to the point! Which happens to be that after Magritte you apparently returned to your car parked in Ponsonby Place, and drove off at the very moment and from the very spot where the escaping minstrel was last observed, which suggests to me that you may have kept a rendezvous and driven off with him in your car.

HARRIS: That is a monstrous allegation, and, it so happens, a lie.

FOOT: Was there any independent witness who can vouch for that?

MOTHER: Yes—there was that man. He waved at me when we were driving off.

FOOT: Can you describe him?

MOTHER: Yes. He was playing hopscotch on the corner, a man in the loose-fitting striped gaberdine of a

38

convicted felon. He carried a handbag under one arm, and with the other he waved at me with a cricket bat.

(FOOT *reels*.)

FOOT: Would you know him again?

MOTHER: I doubt it. He was wearing dark glasses, and a surgical mask.

(HARRIS *comes forward to restore sanity*.)

HARRIS: My mother is a bit confused, Inspector. It was a tortoise under his arm and he wasn't so much playing hopscotch as one-legged.

THELMA: (*deftly slipping the dress over* HARRIS) A tortoise or a football—he was a young man in a football shirt——

HARRIS: *If* I might just stick my oar in here, he could hardly have been a young man since he had a full white beard, and, if I'm not mistaken, side-whiskers.

THELMA: I don't wish to make an issue of this point, but since it has been raised, the energetic if spasmodic hopping of the man's movements hardly suggest someone in his dotage——

HARRIS: I saw him distinctly through the windscreen——

THELMA: It was, of course, raining at the time——

HARRIS: My windscreen wipers were in order, and working——

FOOT: At any rate, regardless of his age, convictions or hobbies, you claim that this man saw you drive off from Ponsonby Place at 2.25 this afternoon?

HARRIS: I'm afraid not, Inspector. He was blind, sweeping a path before him with a white stick——

THELMA: —a West Bromwich Albion squad member, swinging an ivory cane—for goodness sake keep still, Reginald—and get up on the table a minute, my back's breaking——

(HARRIS *mounts the low table, thus easing the angle of* THELMA's *back*.)

HARRIS: My wife is a bit confused——

FOOT: So the best witness you can come up with is a blind, white-bearded, one-legged footballer with a tortoise. How do you account for the animal? Was it a seeing-eye tortoise?

HARRIS: I don't see that the tortoise as such requires explanation. Since the fellow was blind he needn't necessarily have known it was a tortoise. He might have picked it up in mistake for some other object such as a lute.

FOOT: His loot?

HARRIS: Or mandolin.

MOTHER: It was, in fact, an alligator handbag.

FOOT: I'm afraid I can't accept these picturesque fantasies. My wife has an alligator handbag and I defy anyone to mistake it for a musical instrument.

THELMA: *STOP!* Don't move!

(*They desist.*)

I've dropped the needle.

HARRIS: (*looking at his watch*) For God's sake,
Thelma——

THELMA: Help me find it.

(MOTHER *and* FOOT *dutifully get down on their
hands and knees with* THELMA. HARRIS *remains
standing on the table.* MOTHER *and* FOOT *are
head-to-head.*)

MOTHER: Inspector, if the man we saw was blind, who
was the other witness?

FOOT: What other witness?

MOTHER: The one who must have told the police about
our car being there.

FOOT: My dear lady, you have put your finger on one
of the ironies of this extraordinary case. I
myself live at number four Ponsonby Place,
and it was I, glancing out of an upstairs
window, who saw your car pulling away from
the kerb.

MOTHER: And yet, you never saw the minstrel?

FOOT: No, the first I knew about it was when I got to
the station late this afternoon and read the
eye-witness report sent in by the old lady. I
must have missed him by seconds, which led
me to suspect that he had driven off in your
car. I remembered seeing a yellow parking
ticket stuck in your windscreen, and the rest
was child's play.

(*The telephone rings.*)

(*Getting up and going to it.*) Ah—that will be

41

Sergeant Potter. We shall soon see how my
deductions tally with the facts.

(FOOT *picks up the phone. The needle search
continues.* HARRIS *stands, patient and gowned, on
the table.*)

THELMA: Can we have the top light on?

HARRIS: There's no bulb.

THELMA: Get the bulb from the bathroom.

HARRIS: It's gone again.

THELMA: Well, get any bulb!—quickly!

(MOTHER *gets to her one good foot as* FOOT
*replaces the phone dumbstruck and shaken. The
table-lamp is next to the phone.*)

MOTHER: Could you get the bulb out of that lamp,
Inspector?

(FOOT *looks at her unseeingly.*)

The bulb.

(FOOT, *as in a dream, turns to the bulb. His
brain has seized up.*)

You'll need a hanky or a glove.

(FOOT *ineffectually pats his pocket.*)

A woollen sock would do.

(FOOT *sits down wearily and slips off one of his
shoes and his sock.*)

HARRIS: Is something the matter with your foot, Foot?
Inspector, Foot?

(FOOT *thrusts one hand into the woollen sock.
With the other he produces from his pocket a
pair of heavy dark glasses which he puts on.*)

42

You wish to inspect your foot, Inspector?

THELMA: *Can we please have some light?*

FOOT: (*quietly*) Yes—of course—forgive me—I get this awful migraine behind the eyes—it's the shock——

MOTHER: What happened, Inspector?

FOOT: It appears that no robbery of the kind I deduced has in fact taken place among the Victoria Palace Happy Minstrel Troupe. Moreover, there is no minstrel troupe, happy or miserable, playing at that theatre or any other. My reconstruction has proved false in every particular, and it is undoubtedly being voiced back at the station that my past success at deductions of a penetrating character has caused me finally to overreach myself in circumstances that could hardly be more humiliating.

(*They all sense the enormity of it.* HARRIS, *however, is unforgiving. He steps down off the table.*)

THELMA: Oh . . . I'm sorry. Is there anything we can do?

MOTHER: I've always found that bananas are very good for headaches.

HARRIS: (*nastily*) So the crime to which you have accused us of being accessories never in fact took place!

FOOT: That is the position, but before you start congratulating yourself, you still have to explain

43

the incredible and suggestive behaviour witnessed by Constable Holmes through your window.

HARRIS: The activities in this room today have broadly speaking been of a mundane and domestic nature bordering on cliché. Police Constable Holmes obviously has an imagination as fervid and treacherous as your own. If he's found a shred of evidence to back it up then get him in here and let's see it.

FOOT: Very well! (*Calls.*) Holmes!

THELMA: Inspector, the bulb, we need the bulb.

(MOTHER *hops over to the wooden chair by the wall, in order to pick it up, though we do not see her do that.* FOOT'*s attention is still on* HARRIS.)

FOOT: But bear in mind that my error was merely one of interpretation, and whatever did happen in Ponsonby Place this afternoon, your story contains a simple but revealing mistake which clearly indicates that your so-called alibi is a tissue of lies.

HARRIS: What do you mean?

FOOT: You claimed that your witness was a blind one-legged musician.

HARRIS: Roughly speaking.

FOOT: You are obviously unaware that a blind man *cannot stand on one leg*!

HARRIS: Rubbish!

FOOT: It is impossible to keep one's sense of balance

44

for more than a few seconds, and if you don't believe me, try it!

(*Black-out as* FOOT *extracts the bulb.*)

HARRIS: I will!

MOTHER: Over here, Inspector.

(*In the darkness, which for these few seconds should be total,* HARRIS *begins to count, slowly and quietly to himself. But it is* FOOT's *voice that must be isolated.*)

FOOT: The sudden silence as I enter the canteen will be more than I can bear. . . .

MOTHER: Here we are.

FOOT: The worst of it is, if I'd been up a few minutes earlier I could have cracked the case and made the arrest before the station even knew about it.

MOTHER: I'll need the sock.

FOOT: I'd been out with the boys from C Division till dawn, and left my car outside the house, thinking that I'd move it to a parking meter before the wardens came round—in my position one has to set an example, you know. Well, I woke up late and my migraine was giving me hell and my bowels were so bad I had to stop half way through shaving, and I never gave the traffic warden a thought till I glanced out of the window and saw your car pulling away from the only parking space in the road. I flung down my razor and rushed into the street, pausing only to grab my wife's handbag

45

containing the small change and her parasol to
keep off the rain——

MOTHER: You won't mind if I have my practice now,
will you?

FOOT: I got pretty wet because I couldn't unfurl the
damned thing, and I couldn't move fast because
in my haste to pull up my pyjama trousers I
put both feet into the same leg. So after hopping
about a bit and nearly dropping the handbag
into various puddles, I just thought to hell with
it all and went back in the house. My wife
claimed I'd broken her new white parasol, and
when I finally got out of there I had a parking
ticket. I can tell you it's just been one bitch of a
day.

MOTHER: Lights!

THELMA: At last.

(*The central light comes on and the effect is much
brighter. The light has been turned on by* HOLMES
*who stands rooted in the doorway with his hand
still on the switch.*)

(*The row on the table reads from left to right:*

((*1*) MOTHER, *standing on her good foot only, on
the wooden chair which is placed on the table; a
woollen sock on one hand; playing the tuba.*)

((*2*) *Lightshade, slowly descending towards the
table.*)

((*3*) FOOT, *with one bare foot, sunglasses, eating
banana.*)

46

((*4*) *Fruit basket, slowly ascending.*)

((*5*) HARRIS, *gowned, blindfolded with a cushion cover over his head, arms outstretched, on one leg, counting.*)

(THELMA, *in underwear, crawling around the table, scanning the floor and sniffing.*)

(HOLMES *recoils into paralysis.*)

FOOT: Well, Constable, I think you owe us all an explanation.

(*The lampshade descends inexorably as the music continues to play; when it touches the table-top, there is no more light.*)

(*Alternatively, the lampshade could disappear down the horn of the tuba.*)